D1242158

ALVIN BAUMAN

CHARLES W. WALTON

Teachers College, Columbia University

Elementary Musicianship

SECOND EDITION

PRENTICE-HALL, INC. · 1959 · *Englewood Cliffs, N.J.*

PRINTED IN THE UNITED STATES OF AMERICA

25936

Introduction

Music is a language in tone and time and has a vocabulary all its own. In a language, words combine to give content and understanding; so also, the sounds combine to give meaning and significance in music. A language would be limited in scope if we were satisfied to hear successions of words purely for sound's sake and were completely indifferent to its content, its symbols, and meanings. So it is with music. It is not enough to hear music merely as sounds. It is important to understand the symbols, the plan, and the organization of the music. To promote this understanding is the purpose of this book.

The most appropriate place to turn for the study of music is to music itself. Actual music becomes the material for consideration and discussion, not isolated examples completely void of any musical content. The authors feel that an insight into the texture of the music itself is necessary for a meaningful and serviceable understanding of music. As a result, the student is constantly working with music.

This book attempts to present in a clear, nontechnical manner the fundamental aspects of music. There are eleven chapters, and each one is based on an example from music literature which illustrates and explains the point of the lesson. Each new problem is presented through music and in association with that already learned. All types of music have been selected, with the emphasis on the folk song. The rudiments or symbols of music are explained and discussed as the need arises or as they are found in the music. Sufficient material is presented on each new phase of the work for the student to acquire a real working knowledge of the structure of music.

The speed of presentation will depend upon the experience, background, and age of the students and the number of class meetings each week. Certain chapters will need more review and drill than others. The teacher can expand or rearrange the chapters to suit the needs of the students.

The key of C is used exclusively in the first two chapters. Since the material is not intended primarily for writing or the keyboard, it simplifies the initial stages to remain in the same tonality. Beginning with the third chapter, all major keys are used.

The I, IV, V, and V7 chords are discussed as chords whose tones outline skips in the melody. Harmony is used only in the discussion of non-chord tones and when a bass or lower part is added to the melody. The practice and study of the chords, however, lead directly into the first-year theory course.

Music reading is focused on the idea of recognition of patterns in the music: scale-wise progressions, skips of chord tones, and the use of non-chord tones. The analysis of the music becomes very important both aurally and visually. Often music is read note-by-note and interval-by-interval. This handicaps speed in reading and is most unmusical. At first, the analysis is quite simple and general, but it becomes more detailed as the work progresses and the student has more vocabulary.

To give experience in understanding expression and tempo markings, the various symbols are included in some of the melodies. In others, the interpretation is left to the discretion of the performer and the teacher.

Dictation, the process of writing a melody after it is played or sung, is an excellent means of training the ear. The melody should not be dictated or written note-by-note. The student should listen for the general plan of the melody, its form, and then memorize it by phrase.

Too much emphasis cannot be placed on the ear and hearing. Before any discussion or analysis, the music should be performed and listened to attentively. Music depends upon hearing, and one of the chief objectives of this book is to develop intelligent listening, so that understanding of the structure and meanings of music may result.

The authors are greatly indebted to Dr. Howard A. Murphy for his encouragement and valuable suggestions in the preparation of this book.

Grateful acknowledgment is also made to Dr. Charles Haywood for his examination of, and consultation on, the folk song material.

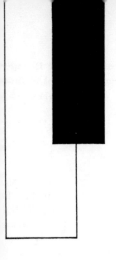

Acknowledgments

Acknowledgment is made to the following publishers and individuals who have granted permission to reprint selections from copyright publications.

APPLETON-CENTURY-CROFTS, INC.
for melodies 26, 31, p. 41; 2, p. 50. *From Sight-Singing Manual,* by Allen Irvine McHose and Ruth Northrup Tibbs. Second edition copyright, 1944, 1945, F. S. Crofts & Co., Inc. Reprinted by permission of the publishers.

ASSOCIATED MUSIC PUBLISHERS, INC.
for melody example 59, p. 52. From *Das Lied des Volker,* vol. V, ed. by Heinrich Moeller. Copyright, 1926. Reprinted by permission of the publishers.

BEHRMAN HOUSE, INC., PUBLISHERS
for melody 23, p. 207. "Hannukkah Song," from *The Gateway to Jewish Song,* by Judith Einstein. Reprinted by permission of the publishers.

CROWN PUBLISHERS
for melodies 6-18, pp. 102-106; 27, p. 109; 11, p. 130; 15, p. 132. From *A Treasury of the World's Finest Folk Song,* ed. Leonhard Deutsch. Copyright, 1942, Leonhard Deutsch. Reprinted by permission of the publishers.

E. P. DUTTON & CO., INC.
for melodies 10, p. 67; 19-20, p. 106. From *Canadian Folk Songs, Old and New,* by J. Murray Gibson. Copyright, 1927. Reprinted by permission of the publishers.

HAROLD FLAMMER, INCORPORATED
for melodies 6-7, p. 11. From *First Studies in Harmonic Analysis.* Copyright, 1925. Reprinted by permission of the publishers.

FOLKWAYS RECORDS
for melody 3, p. 18. From record #FC7003 (FP703). Used by permission of the publishers.

GINN AND COMPANY
for melody 4, p. 15. From *Singing and Rhyming* of *Our Singing World* series. Copyright, Ginn and Company. Reprinted by permission of the publishers.

Contents

Notation

Old song

Andante

1

Sing and learn this simple folk song with the syllables loo or la. These musical tones or sounds are represented on paper by certain marks, signs, and figures (symbols). This representation is called *musical notation*. Our system of notation has been developed over many centuries and serves as a means for the composer to present his ideas in a permanent and communicable way.

Let us now analyze and study the notation of this melody and discover what the various symbols mean.

1. The five horizontal lines are called a *staff*:

2

2. Tones are represented by *notes* (♩ ♩) which are placed on the lines and spaces of the staff. Notice some are on the lines and some are on the spaces between the lines.

Sing this melody again and follow the notes as you sing. Notice the up and down movement of the melody.

3. At the beginning of the staff there is a symbol or sign (𝄞). This is called the *clef sign* and identifies the names and pitches of the notes on the staff. This one is called the *treble* or *G clef* and locates the note G on the staff. Without this clef sign, the staff and the notes are meaningless. Other clef signs are used in music and we will discuss them as they appear in our melodies.

4. As we discovered earlier, the tones you have been singing are represented by notes placed on the lines and spaces of the staff. In the first melody, notice that the first note is on an added line below the staff. This added line below (or sometimes above) the staff is called a *leger line*. Letters of the alphabet (A to G) are assigned to the tones or pitches. As we mentioned previously, the G clef locates the tone or letter G (second line) on the staff. Notice how the line of the clef crosses this line three times. By counting down from G we find that the first tone of this melody is C. This is called *middle C* on the piano. The first five tones of the melody are on adjacent lines and spaces, and, therefore, follow in alphabetical order: C, D, E, F, G ascending and G, F, E, D, C descending.

Here is the same melody with letters and numbers. Sing it several times and listen carefully to the sound as you sing. Use letter names, loo or la, and numbers. Notice these five notes are repeated several times. This repetition adds unity to the music.

On the piano chart below, locate these five tones and hear them on the piano. They are five consecutive white keys on the piano.

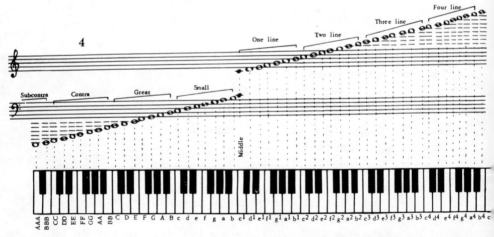

Courtesy of Raymond Elliott, *Fundamentals of Music*
(Englewood Cliffs, N.J.: Prentice-Hall, Inc., 1955).

2

Danish folk song

Sing and learn this second folk song and compare it to the first one. Notice the same five tones are used but in a different arrangement. The beginning tone here is E. How many times does C occur? Find the other four tones. Several of the tones are repeated. Sing with letter names and listen carefully as you sing. Find these notes on the piano chart.

In singing these melodies, what tone seems to be the most prominent or the one which makes the melody sound complete? All the other tones seem drawn or pulled to C each time for a complete or final ending. This central tone is called the *key tone.* This relationship of a series of tones to a key or "home" tone gives us *tonality* in music. *Tonal music,* therefore, is music which bases its organization on the predominance of this key tone.

RHYTHM

As you have sung these melodies, you have no doubt noticed that certain tones are longer in duration than others and that some tones seem to receive more stress. Sing the Ex. 1 melody again and clap or tap with the notes you sing. The tones or notes are grouped together in various patterns. The effect produced by this grouping of tones is called *rhythm* in music. In examining the music further, we find perpendicular lines on the staff throughout the melody. These are called *bar lines* and divide the staff into *measures.* These measures help to clarify the rhythmic pattern of a melody. The *double bar* at the end of the melody marks the close or end of the melody. Underlying the rhythm of the music (the duration of tones) is a basic scheme of pulses or beats within each measure which remains unaltered and which serves as a skeleton for the rhythm. These pulses or beats (a fixed unit of time) can be compared to the regular recurrent heart beat or the steady monotonous beat of the drum. This effect is called *meter* in music. For example, sing the familiar song *America.* Tap or clap the regular recurrent beat as you sing the melody. Your clapping or tapping is the meter of the music, and the grouping of the tones of the melody forms the rhythm.

The exact length of tones in rhythm is indicated in the notation by various kinds of notes, and by *stems* and *flags* or *hooks* on the notes. To give these notes meaning and to set up a pattern for the meter of the music, we find two numbers written vertically at the beginning of the melody. This symbol is the *time signature.* The upper number indicates the number of beats in the measure, and the lower one indicates the kind of note that receives one beat, that is, the unit of measurement.

3

In the time signature of the first melody (Ex. 1), we see the top number is 4. This means that there are four beats or pulses within the measure. Clap or tap four beats to a measure and sing the melody. Tap a full measure before singing. It is also excellent practice to conduct the music as you sing. The outline for conducting four beats to a measure is thus:

6

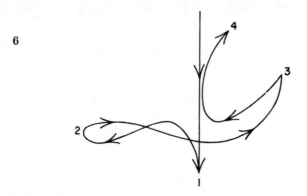

You have been conducting the meter of the music and singing the rhythm. Which note receives one tap or one movement of the arm in conducting? The *quarter note* (♩). In this song, then, the quarter note receives one beat which is indicated in the time signature by the lower 4. In the first measure of the melody, there are four quarter notes and each receives one beat, thus completing the four pulses of the measure. In contrast to measure one, the first note in measure 2 receives two beats. This is held twice as long as the quarter note and so it is called a *half note* (♩). In measure 4 there is only one note. It, therefore, receives four beats and is a *whole note* (○).

Here is a diagram of the meter and the rhythm of the melody:

7

Rhythm: **4/4** ♩♩♩♩ | ♩ ♩ | ♩♩♩♩ | ○ | ♩♩♩♩ | ♩ ♩ | ♩♩♩♩ | ○ ‖

Meter: ♩♩♩♩ | ♩♩♩♩ | ♩♩♩♩ | ♩♩♩♩ | ♩♩♩♩ | ♩♩♩♩ | ♩♩♩♩ | ♩♩♩♩ ‖
1 2 3 4 | 1 2 3 4 | 1 2 3 4 | 1 2 3 4 | 1 2 3 4 | 1 2 3 4 | 1 2 3 4 | 1 2 3 4 ‖

Sing this melody again and notice that there is a natural stress or slight accent on the first beat of each measure. The recurrence of rhythmic patterns often makes the first beat more prominent. However, this stress should be considered a tendency and not a rigid procedure, since its use can easily separate the melody into small unmusical groupings, which hinder the natural flow and beauty of the melody.

Sing and conduct the melody (Ex. 5) on page 3 again. Notice the rhythmic similarities to the first melody. What is the rhythmic plan of measures 4 and 8? In these measures there is a half note followed by a dot. A quarter note completes the measure. In conducting or tapping the rhythm of the melody, you probably discovered that the half note and dot receive three beats. We already know that with a time signature of 4/4, the half note receives two beats, so obviously the dot receives one beat, making the total of three. This, therefore, shows us that a dot following a note adds one-half the value of the note.

Sing and examine the above melody. In the first measure there are three quarter notes and then two notes connected by a line or beam. In conducting this measure, you will discover that the two notes (♫) receive one beat. Thus the quarter note beat is divided into two equal parts and the notes are called *eighth notes* (♪). Sometimes they are joined together in groups by beams or ligatures as in our example, and sometimes they are written separately with flags or hooks.*

Summary of notes

Whole   𝅝

Half   𝅗𝅥

Dotted half   𝅗𝅥.

Quarter   ♩

Eighth   ♪

---

* The connection of notes by beams (♫) in vocal music indicates that they are to be sung to one syllable of the words. If each note has a different syllable, separate flags are used (♪ ♪). Since there are no words to most of the music in this book, the beams are used to join the notes in groups of beats or pulses. This greatly simplifies the reading of the rhythm.

10   ♫
      we__
    ♪ ♪
   walk - ing

Suggestions for study

1. Conduct the meter as you sing.
2. Sing with letter names, loo or la.
3. Keep in mind the five-note pattern.
4. Copy several of the melodies for practice in writing music.
5. After singing the melodies several times, see how much of the melody you can write on the staff from memory.
6. Practice drawing the G clef and the various kinds of notes.
7. Review the five notes so you can recognize them quickly in any context.
8. Find these same notes in other music.
9. Refer often to the piano chart.
10. Analyze the melodies for repetitions of measures and similar patterns.

In some of the melodies the time signature is 2/4 instead of 4/4. This naturally means that there are two beats or pulses to a measure and a quarter note receives one beat. In conducting this meter the outline is thus:

11

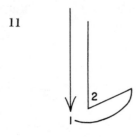

Certain Italian words at the beginning of the melodies inform the performer of the speed or *tempo* of the music. Here is a short list of the most common ones you will need in the following melodies.

Andante: Moderately slow.
Allegretto: Moderately fast.
Moderato: At a moderate rate of speed.
Allegro: Lively, rapid.
Andantino: A little faster than andante.
Largo: Slow.
Marcato: Marked or accented.

MELODIES FOR SINGING AND DICTATION

1. British folk song

Moderato

2. Folk song of eastern Europe

Andante

3. French folk song

Allegro

4. Old round

Lively

Moderato

6. Mozart, Horn Sextet K 522

Allegro marcato

7. Beethoven, Piano Concerto No. 5, first movement

Allegro

8. Old church melody

Andante

9. English singing game

Gaily

Sing the first part of the song *America*. Here is the rhythmic outline:

Notice the time signature is 3/4. We now have three beats to the measure and the conducting pattern is:

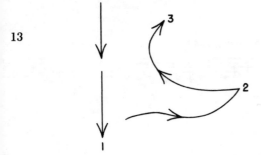

In measures 2 and 4 there is a dotted quarter note followed by an eighth note (♩. ♪). You have sung this rhythm in this song many times. Analyze it more closely and compare the rhythm with the words.

14

1	2	3	1 2 & 3	1	2	3	1 2 & 3	1	2	3	1 2 3
My	coun-	try	'tis of Thee,	Sweet	land	of	li - ber-ty,	Of	Thee	I	sing.

9

Conduct the three beats to a measure and sing first the words, then sing counting the rhythm, one, two, three, and so on. On what part of the measure does the dot come? Notice in measure 2 the word "tis" is sung on the first beat and carries over into the first part of the second beat. The syllable "of" comes in and completes the second beat, and "thee" finishes the measure. Test this pattern again, conducting and singing. Here again, as in our other experiences with the dot, it receives one-half the value of the note it follows.

15   ♩. ♪ ♩
   1 ♪ ♪ 1
   1 2 & 3

Note: Sometimes two dots are used following a note. Here the second dot receives one-half the value of the first dot.

MELODIES FOR SINGING AND DICTATION

Insert bar lines in the first two melodies.

1. English singing game

With spirit

2. Beethoven, Symphony No. 9, last movement

Allegro

3. Schumann, Carnaval, Op. 9

Largo

4. Folk song from Humperdinck, Hansel and Gretel

Swinging rhythm

5. Syrian folk song

Allegro

6. Folk song

Moderato

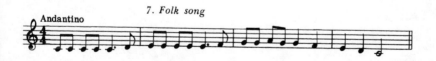

7. Folk song

Andantino

11

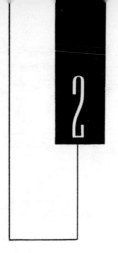

The Major Scale

Here is the notation for the first part of the Christmas carol, *The First Nowell*. Sing it and follow the notes as you sing.* Where does the first main accent or stress come? It is on the third note of the melody on the word "first." The first two notes are only part of a full measure and are equal to one beat (♩♩), the third beat of the incomplete measure. In conducting this melody the first two notes are sung while the hand is moving up for the third beat with the main accent coming on the down beat. 3/123/ and so on. This is called an *upbeat* or an *anacrusis* in music. Many melodies begin on an upbeat or an incomplete measure as we will discover.

Some of the notes of the above melody you will easily recognize. Notice the similarities to the melodies previously studied. Find the five-note pattern

---

* Note that when the words are used with the melody, the two consecutive eighth notes singing the same syllable are joined by a beam (♫); when they each have a different syllable or word, they are separated (♪ ♪) (see measure four).

at the beginning of the melody. There are, however, several unfamiliar notes in the music. In measure 2 the G (half note) progresses up to the adjacent space and on to the next line and the next space. Thus we have three new tones or notes and they follow the same alphabetical plan as before: A, B, C. Find these new notes on the piano chart (Ex. 4, p. 2); they are the white keys of the piano. We now have the pitches or tones on adjacent lines and spaces from C to C. This completes a step-wise arrangement of eight tones. When the tones are arranged in this order (the first two measures of the melody), they form a *scale,* which is from the Latin word scala, meaning ladder. This scale from C to C ascending and descending is called a *major scale* because of its tonal pattern. Sing the scale with letter names and loo or la several times and listen to it carefully. The scale begins on C and progresses up to C; this space from C to C is called an *octave.* The top C is an octave above or higher than the lower C.

Scale of C

17

These tones all belong to the tonality of C major and C is the key tone. All the tones belonging to the key tone or tonality are called *diatonic tones.*

Now consider the relationship of these tones to each other, that is, the *interval* relationship. An *interval* is the difference in pitch or the distance on the staff between any two tones. We are at present interested in the relationship between C and D, D and E and so on up the scale. Since the sounds are heard consecutively, they form *melodic intervals.* Refer again to the piano chart and notice the octave from C to C. Above the white keys you will find groups of two and three black keys. Progressing up or down from any black or white key to the nearest black or white key is an interval of a *half step.* Two half steps combine to make a *whole step.* By starting on middle C and progressing up, we see the tones of our C major scale are made up of either whole or half steps. The half steps come between the 3rd and 4th degrees of the scale and between the 7th and 8th degrees of the scale. The others are whole steps.

18

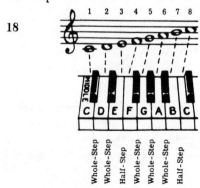

The seven tones of the scale are named as follows: C tonic; D super tonic; E mediant; F subdominant; G dominant; A submediant; B leading tone.

Sing this new melody and study it carefully. By now all the notes should be familiar to you. Notice the ascending scale in the first four measures. What other measures use the scale? In measures 5 and 8 there is a new part or section of the melody which is repeated in the following four measures. The melody closes with the scale again. The first part (we can call it *A*) is the scale; then we have new material (*B*) which is repeated, and then the scale again (*A*). Thus, there are three parts to this melody. The arrangement of musical material and the plan or organization of the music is called *form*. This, therefore, is a *three-part form* (*ABA*). The repetition of *A* gives unity and balance to the melody; the new material offers variety and contrast. In all music there should be a balance between unity and variety for music to sound well. Form will be discussed in more detail in Chapter 11.

Notice the form and design of each melody as you study it. As you sing and analyze the melodies, be conscious of repetitions and new material in the music. Your reading skill will be greatly improved by observing and analyzing all music you see and hear in regard to scale-wise progressions, repeated tones, repetitions of patterns, and so on. It is an excellent idea to go back constantly and review previous melodies so that they may become more a part of your music vocabulary.

Additional terms

Larghetto: Not as slow as largo.
Con anima: With animation and boldness.

In some of the melodies, you will find the symbol ⌒ over certain notes. This is called a *fermata* or *hold* in music and indicates that the tone is to be prolonged or held. The duration depends upon the type of music and the musical taste of the performer or conductor. It is used in the type of hymn tune known as the *chorale*.

MELODIES FOR SINGING AND DICTATION

1. British folk song

Allegretto

2. Beethoven, Trio Op. 1, No. 3, first movement

3. Mozart, Hostias from Requiem Mass

Larghetto

4. Louise Gliere, Bonfire

Allegro

From *Singing and Rhyming* of *Our Singing World*
series. Used by permission of Ginn and Company,
owner of the copyright.

5. Bach

Moderato

6. British folk song

Allegretto

Music would be quite limited and monotonous if all the tones available to a composer were in this one octave from middle C to the C above. We can see by the piano chart that there are other octaves higher and lower which offer variety in tone and color. Thus we could begin the melody (Ex. 19) on page 14 on the third line of the staff (C) and place all the notes an octave higher. The same letters are used and leger lines are needed above the staff to complete the scale. Here is the melody an octave higher: *

Refer to the piano chart (p. 2) and locate this higher octave and scale. Find the other C's and octaves on the chart. Practice and study these tones so you will recognize them in your music.

Sing the first part of *Joy to the World.* Notice the complete descending scale and part of the ascending one. If we wanted to write this melody an octave lower starting the scale on middle C and continuing on down through the next octave, we would have to use many leger lines and the reading would become quite difficult. To avoid this problem, another clef sign is used: the *bass* or *F clef.*

22 𝄢 This clef locates F on the fourth line. Notice the curved part of the clef circles this line. By counting up from F we find that C is located on the first leger line above the staff. This is the same C in sound

---

* Stems on the notes are placed down, beginning with the third line of the staff and on all the notes above the third line.

as middle C so the clefs converge at this point. *Joy to the World* would then
be written this way an octave lower using the F clef:

23

C   B A   G   F   E   D   C   G   A   A   B   B   C

Instruments or voices of higher pitch use the G clef while those of lower
pitch use the F clef. The pianist uses both clefs which combine to form a
Grand Staff. Refer to the piano chart again and see how the tones of the

24   **Grand Staff**

two clefs combine and merge into a continuous system. The brace which
combines the two clefs indicates that the music is to be performed simultaneously. These two clefs are the most common and the most widely used
ones. Another one, the C or alto Clef is used for certain orchestral instruments. Here middle C is on the third line:

25

We have now found the tones and their names for three octaves. The
others can be learned as they appear in our music. Learn these notes and
their names thoroughly.

26

C   D   E   F   G   A   B   C   D   E   F   G   A   B   C   D   E   F   G   A   B   C

Note: Sometimes the symbol 8va . . . . is placed over several notes. This
is an abbreviation for all' ottavo, which indicates that all the tones are to be
performed an octave higher. When the sign is used below the staff, it indicates that the tones are to be performed an octave lower. The term 8va
. . . . bassa is sometimes used. These symbols avoid the use of leger lines
and greatly simplify the notation.

MELODIES FOR SINGING AND DICTATION *

1. Old song

Moderately fast

2. English folk song†

3. I Walk Upstairs—Children's street game

---

* If the melodies are out of range of the voice, transfer the tones up or down an octave.

---

† Sometimes the symbols C and ¢ are used for the time signatures 4/4 and 2/2 respectively. In sixteenth-century notation, music in triple meter (three pulses) was indicated by a circle: O Music that was not in triple meter was indicated by a broken circle: C The name for ¢ is *alla breve*, which refers to an early note value.

18

4. English folk song

5. Bach, Chorale melody

6. Chorale melody

7. Chorale melody

8. Beethoven, Piano Sonata Op. 53, first movement

Allegro

9. Cruger, Now Thank We All Our God

Slowly

19

10. Czechoslovakian folk song

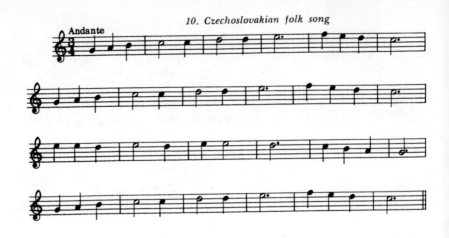

11. Bach

12. Old English song

13. Bartok

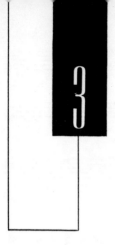

Keys and Signatures

In singing and writing the scale, we have thus far always started and ended on C. This is the *C major scale*. Let us now examine some other possibilities. Beginning on C, sing the first four measures of *Joy to the World*, the descending scale. Now sing the same scale beginning on G. When this is played on the piano, you will find it is impossible to have the same sound as the major scale by playing the white keys from G to G as was done on C. By experimenting a bit we find the tone F needs to be altered for our ears to be satisfied. The black key above and to the right of the white key makes the necessary adjustment for our ears. Since it is above the F, the F tone is raised or "sharped," and the sharp sign (♯) is placed in front of the note on the staff. Thus, when the scale is written beginning on G, the F sharp is used ascending and descending. This is the *G major scale* and the tone G becomes the key tone and the center of a new tonality. Try the scale again, beginning on F this time. When it is played on the piano, we find that the B needs some adjustment and the ear soon discovers that the correct tone is the black tone directly below the B. Since it is below, the B is lowered or "flatted," and the flat sign (♭) is placed in front of the note on the staff.*
This is the *F major scale*.

Here are the major scales of C, G, and F. Notice the whole and half steps are the same in these scales. This organization is consistent in all major scales.

---

* The double flat (♭♭) or double sharp (𝄪) represents a pitch one whole step lower or higher respectively.

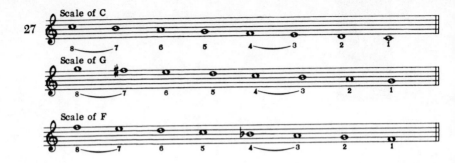

Locate these three scales on the piano chart, p. 2 , as you sing them and as they are played on the piano. As previously mentioned, the black keys are arranged in groups of twos and threes above the white keys. Thus, within one octave from C to C, we have twelve different pitches. Hear the tones, sing them, and follow the notation. These tones form the *chromatic scale* and will be discussed later in the chapter on chromaticism. Here is the chromatic scale from C to C:

It is possible to form a major scale on any of these tones by using all the black and white keys. Each one of these pitches or tones can become the key tone of the particular scale or group of tones. Each one can be found and worked out by ear in the same manner as was done with G and F.

In writing a melody in the key of G, the sharp sign would appear before each F in the notation. To avoid this constant repetition and to show the reader of the music that the melody is in the key of G, and that all the F's are sharped, a sharp sign is placed at the beginning of the melody on the line F before the time signature:

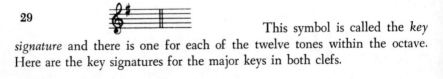

This symbol is called the *key signature* and there is one for each of the twelve tones within the octave. Here are the key signatures for the major keys in both clefs.

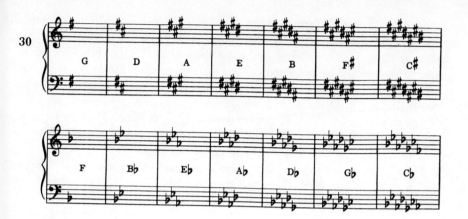

Here is an outline of the scales and their corresponding sharps or flats. These keys will all be represented in our melodies throughout the book. Study them carefully and practice writing the key signatures on the staff.

SCALE

31

C							
G	F♯						
D	F♯	C♯					
A	F♯	C♯	G♯				
E	F♯	C♯	G♯	D♯			
B	F♯	C♯	G♯	D♯	A♯		
F♯	F♯	C♯	G♯	D♯	A♯	E♯	
C♯	F♯	C♯	G♯	D♯	A♯	E♯	B♯
F	B♭						
B♭	B♭	E♭					
E♭	B♭	E♭	A♭				
A♭	B♭	E♭	A♭	D♭			
D♭	B♭	E♭	A♭	D♭	G♭		
G♭	B♭	E♭	A♭	D♭	G♭	C♭	
C♭	B♭	E♭	A♭	D♭	G♭	C♭	F♭

In examining and learning these key signatures and scales, you will find, for example, that the key of B (five sharps) and C flat (seven flats) use the same pitches. The key tone B is the same sound as C flat. Thus each pitch can be represented by two letters. E flat is the same sound as D sharp, G flat as F sharp, etc. This double spelling is called *enharmonic notation*. When E flat is changed to D sharp for musical reasons, it is changed *enharmonically*. Thus, theoretically, all scales can be written enharmonically, but only three are commonly used: C flat (B), G flat (F sharp), and D flat (C sharp). We have, then, seven sharp keys and seven flat keys.

Here is an arrangement of these keys in relation to the number of sharps and flats in the signature. Note that each is a fifth tone higher, progressing clock-wise.

32

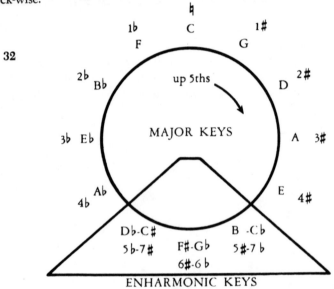

Adapted from Walter Ehret, Lawrence Barr, and Elizabeth Blair, *Time for Music* (Englewood Cliffs. N.J.: Prentice-Hall, Inc., 1959).

Sing several of the previous melodies and write them in other keys for practice. Write all the major scales, using the necessary sharps or flats with the notes.* After each scale place the corresponding key signature. For example:

33

---

* When the sharp and flat signs are employed throughout a melody, they are called *accidentals*. If a sharp or flat notated in the key signature is to be cancelled during a melody, a natural sign (♮) is used. All accidentals affect only the exact pitch they precede and only those same pitches within the measure in which they appear.

24

Test each one with the ear and learn them thoroughly. When the key is changed from one to the other, we say the melody is *transposed*. This becomes necessary when the voice or instrument is higher or lower in pitch. It is a shifting of tonal patterns to different tone levels.

Sing this folk song. What is the key? In examining the notation you will find several curved lines ———————— throughout the melody. This line has two meanings:

1. Notice the curved line joining the two notes of the upbeat. It is called a *slur,* and it connects or binds together a group of notes of different pitches. It indicates that these tones are to be performed in a connected and smooth manner. The Italian term *legato* has the same meaning and is closely associated with this symbol. Find the other slur markings in this melody.
2. In measures 7-8 a similar line ——— connects two (or more) notes of the same pitch. This line is called a *tie,* and indicates that the sound is to be continuous and equal in time to the sum of all the notes joined together. The tones are not repeated but are held their full value. The tie is also found in the last two measures.

You will notice several other signs and symbols in the music which offer certain suggestions and which assist us in the performance of the music. These indications are, of course, relative, as meanings and interpretations of terms and symbols differ with each composer, conductor and performer. However, they do serve as valuable guides in the interpretation and performance of the music. Here are the symbols found in this melody.

Tempo symbols

1. Andante: Moderately slow.
2. *Rit.*: Abbreviation of *ritardando,* gradually slower or a gradual delaying.

Expression symbols

1. *p:* Abbreviation for *piano,* meaning "softly."
2. ◁ Gradually becoming louder. The term *crescendo* (*cres.*) has the same meaning.
3. ▷ Decreasing in power. The word *decrescendo* (*decreas.*) is often used.
4. 𝄐 The dot above or below a note indicates that the tones are to be performed in a detached or separated manner. This is called *staccato* and is in direct contrast to the term *legato.*

Some additional symbols in the following melodies

1. *mf: Mezzo forte,* moderately loud.
2. *f: Forte,* strong, loud.
3. > Stress or emphasis. Also sometimes *sforzando* written *sfz.*
4. *dim: diminuendo,* diminishing tone power.
5. 𝄐 This short line above or below a note is a *portato* and indicates a non-legato tone but not as short as staccato.
6. *Lento:* Slow.

MELODIES FOR SINGING AND DICTATION

1. British folk song

2. English folk song

3. Caldara, Canon for three voices

26

4. Schumann, Chorale from Album for the Young

5. Bach, Chorale melody

6. Folk song

7. Chorale melody

8. Chorale melody

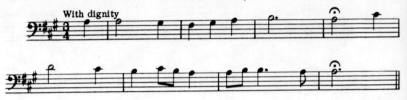

9. Folk song

The Tonic Chord

MELODIC LINE

Sing and examine this melody. Look it over for familiar and similar patterns. Measures 2-4 use the five tones of the descending scale with repeated tones. Where else in the melody is this pattern found? Measures 9-11 have the five-note pattern ascending. Notice that the first three tones of this melody are skips within this five-note pattern. Our previous melodies have been mainly scale-wise. This is the first time we have had skips in the melody. The tones here are on alternate lines of the staff.

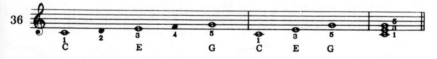

These three tones (C, E, G) are called a *triad*. The C is the root of the triad, and, counting upward from the root, the E is the third and the G the fifth. Since C is the root of the triad and since it is the first degree of the scale, the triad or chord is called the *I chord*. Chords are named by Roman numerals. This triad or chord is a most important one and will be outlined in our melodies both ascending and descending many times. In what other measures is the I chord outlined? Notice all the skips are between C, E and G.

Sing the I chord in outline form in all keys using letter names and accidentals. The chord is in *arpeggio form* when the tones of the chord are sung or played in succession. Notice the root is repeated to complete the octave.

Hungarian folk song

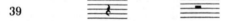

Sing and analyze this melody. Here again we have the skips of the I chord and the key is G major. There are several symbols in the melody which may need some clarification for a more accurate reading of the music. A composer will often designate pauses or places of silence in music to create certain desired effects. This is indicated by the use of signs or symbols called *rests*. These rests are placed on the staff to show the length of the silence. The various types of rests follow the same time duration as their corresponding notes.

In the first measure of the melody above, the symbol is a *quarter rest* (𝄽). In the fourth measure the short line on the third line of the staff is a *half rest* (━). Locate these two rests throughout this melody and pay close attention to them as you sing. The feeling and expressiveness of the music are often dependent on the proper use and performance of these rests.

In measures 8-9 of the following melody we find a whole measure of silence. This symbol is a *whole rest.**

This is a good review melody.

Palestrina

---

* Consecutive silent measures are often indicated in the score by this symbol with the number of silent measures:

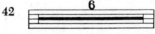

In singing this melody, notice that in measures 4, 5, and 15 the second beat (♩) receives a slight stress because of its length. Thus the stress is on the second beat (normally a weak beat) rather than the usual first beat. When the normal stress is upset this way, we have *syncopation* in music.

Haydn, Symphony in C Major

In looking over this melody we find another symbol of the rest (𐐒). This is an eighth rest and corresponds in length to the eighth note. Sing this melody and give particular attention to the rests.

British folk song

In the above melody there are skips of the I chord and step-wise movement. We have seen that many of our melodies follow a definite scale pattern ascending and descending. When the tones do not move along in this scale-wise progression up and down, they have certain resolutions which sound most natural and agreeable to our ears. We have previously discovered that the key or central tone gives a feeling of rest or completeness. The other tones of the I chord (third and fifth) are also tones of rest. They are more or less inactive and do not demand resolution or movement to another tone. The other tones of the scale (2, 4, 6, and 7) are active tones and create a motion or pull to a rest or inactive tone. These active tones have a tendency to resolve in a certain way. They are illustrated in this example. For instance, in measure 1, the 6th degree moves to 5; in measure 6, the 4th to 3; in measures 12-13, the 7th to the key tone or tonic, and in the next to last measure the 2nd moves to 1. Test these resolutions in singing and at the piano.

Here is a summary of the tones and their resolutions:

The time signatures in our melodies have all been either 2/4, 3/4 or 4/4. In some of the melodies that follow, the lowest number in the time signature is 2, meaning that the half note (♩) is the basic unit of measurement and receives one beat or pulse in the measure. We can now add 4/2, 2/2, and 3/2 to our time signatures. All of these time signatures we have discovered in the music represent *simple meters*, since a beat or pulse can be divided by two or its multiples.

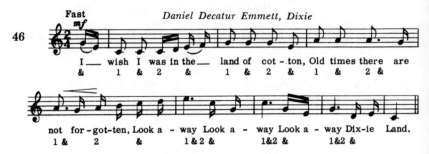

Sing the first eight measures of *Dixie* and notice the rhythm as you sing. The upbeat at the beginning of the melody outlines the I chord. In conducting the meter of the first measure, you will find that the two eighth notes receive one beat and the following four notes with the double flags receive the second and final beat of the measure. Thus these four notes make up one beat or pulse ( ). The beat is subdivided and the notes are called *sixteenth notes*. Notice also sixteenth notes are used on the upbeat, so the melody begins on the second half of the second beat. Since the beat is subdivided, it is practical and perhaps more simple at first to use the word "and" in counting the second part of the pulse. This is done in the example. The second measure has four even eighth notes. In the third measure there are two eighth notes followed by a dotted eighth and sixteenth note. This is a most common rhythmic pattern in music. Sing this rhythm several times conducting and clapping. Learn the sound of the rhythm, so you will be able to sing it and locate it in other music. In measures 5 and 6, notice again the skips of the I chord and the dotted quarter followed by two sixteenth notes. All the tones of the C major scale are in this melody. The melody, then, consists of scale-wise progressions, skips of chord tones and repeated tones. These are all the possibilities of any melody.

In this melody, *Taps*, the dotted eighth and sixteenth note pattern is used frequently. Sing this melody and notice the skips of the I chord in G major.

The melody below presents another rhythmic pattern using the sixteenth note. In measures 3 and 4, the sixteenth notes are joined to an eighth note.

In measure 9 in Example 49, sixteenth rests are used. Find the other rests in the melody, and pay close attention to them as you sing.

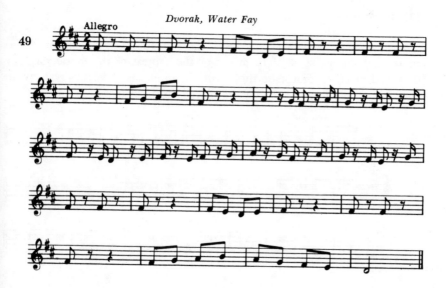

Summary of sixteenth note possibilities

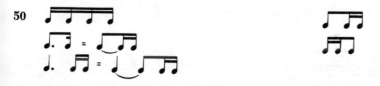

Summary of notes and their corresponding rests

Whole note   o   ▬

Half note   ♩   ▬

Quarter note   ♩   ✷

Eighth note   ♪   ❼

Sixteenth note   ♪   ❼

Simple meters

2/4; 3/4; 4/4; 4/2; 2/2; 3/2.

Terms

Allegro di molto: Very quick and animated.
Con spirito: With spirit and energy.
Poco: A little.

We have discovered that the skips of the I chord are used in many different ways. Here are some of them out of the context of the music for your study and practice. Transpose these patterns to all major keys. Try to write them down from memory as they are played on the piano.

51

MELODIES FOR SINGING AND DICTATION

1. Haydn, Melody

2. Mozart, Gavotte

3. Reveille, U. S. bugle call

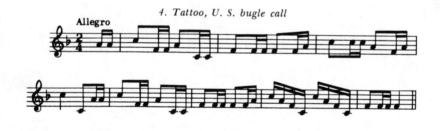

4. Tattoo, U. S. bugle call

5. Handel, Amen Chorus from the Messiah

6. American play song

7. U. S. bugle call

8. Mess, U. S. bugle call

9. Assembly, U. S. bugle call

10. Dutch folk song

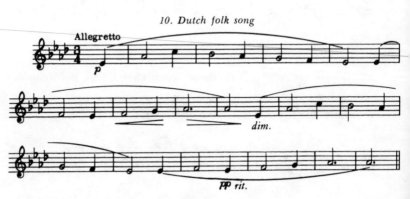

11. German folk song

Moderato

mf

cresc.

f

dim.

12. Clementi, Rondo from Sonata No. 5

Allegro

13. British folk song

Moderato

p

f

dim.

p

14. British folk song

Moderato

mf

p

15. German folk song

16. Breton folk song

17. German folk song

18. French folk song

19. German folk song

20. German folk song

21. Latin folk song

22. Swiss folk song

23. Eastern Europe song

24. W. Otto Meissner, The Fruit Peddler

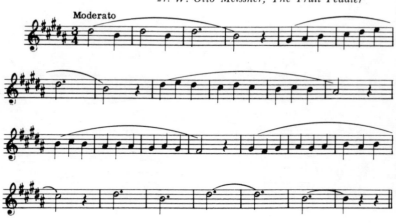

25. German chorale melody

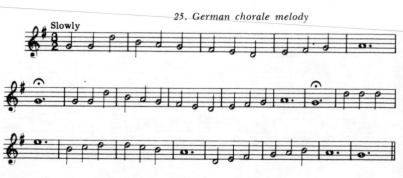

40

26. Arabian folk song

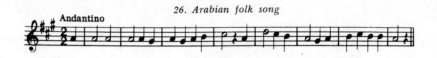

27. German folk song

28. Dutch folk song

29. Dutch folk song

30. British folk song

31. Bohemian folk song

32. German folk song

33. German folk song

34. British folk song

35. Hungarian folk song

36. German folk song

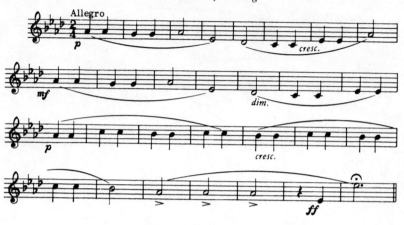

37. French folk song

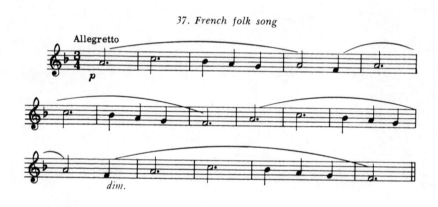

38. Clementine

39. British folk song

40. German folk song

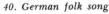

41. German folk song

42. Russian folk song

43. German folk song

44. German folk song

Andante

45. British folk song

Allegretto

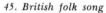

46. Gluck, Air de Ballet

47. Russian folk song

Allegretto

48. German folk song

Allegretto

45

49. 17th century hymn

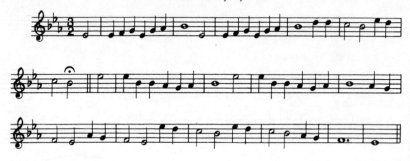

50. Swedish folk song

51. Serbian folk song

52. German folk song

53. Hungarian folk song

54. Bach, Chorale

55. Bach, Chorale

56. Bach, Chorale

57. Bach, Chorale

47

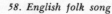

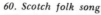

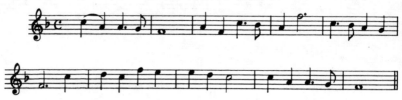

The Dominant Chord

German folk song

German folk song

With spirit

52

Sing and analyze this folk melody. Notice the scale-wise progressions, the skips, and the repeated notes. In the fifth measure, there are skips on adjacent spaces with D as the lowest tone or root.

53

meas. 5   V¹

Here we have a triad or chord with tones on adjacent spaces. D is the root of the chord, F sharp is the third, and A the fifth. Since D is the root of the chord and it is the fifth degree of the scale, the chord is the *V chord*. Notice the D is a tone in both the I and V chords.

54

I   V   V   V

Sing with letter names and accidentals the I and V chords in all keys. Refer back to the folk song for review. Write the I and V chords in all keys in arpeggio form.

49

55
I   V   I

MELODIES FOR SINGING AND DICTATION

1. Old song

Slowly

2. Polish folk song

Andantino

3. German folk song

Waltz time

4. Folk song from Yugoslavia

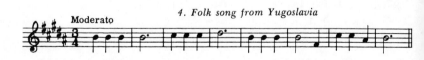

Moderato

5. English folk song

Andante

The skips of the tones of the V chord will be found many times in our music. The I and V chords are the two most frequently used chords in music. By singing these chords in all keys and by becoming familiar with them, the reading of new melodies will be greatly aided both in speed and accuracy.

Swinging   *German folk song*

56

Sing and analyze the above melody. Notice all the skips in the melody outline either the I or the V chord. By singing the root of the two chords (G or D) at the proper place, we can sing a very simple accompaniment to the melody. In this way a second part is added. While the melody is being played on the piano, try singing either G or D (one tone to each measure for the present) and decide where the tones sound best. Here is an outline of the added part with one tone to each measure.

$$\frac{3}{4} \text{ G / G / D / G / G / D / G / D / G / D / G / G / D / G / /}$$

Divide the class and sing both parts. When the melody outlines the I chord, the root of the I chord (G) is best. The root of the V (D) is used when the V chord is outlined. Notice V to I in the last two measures. This progression at the end of a melody is called a *cadence*. A cadence of V to I is called an *authentic cadence.* When the last note of the melody is the key tone, the cadence is a *perfect authentic one.* Check on the endings or cadences in other melodies.

When the I and V chords are played on the piano, we have this pattern:

Notice the step-wise movement of these tones and that the root is doubled in each chord which is the usual procedure when chords are played or sung. While these chords are being played on the piano, the class should sing the melody. Thus we have an accompaniment to the melody. Find these chords on the piano chart (p. 2) and try writing them in other keys. Divide the class and sing these chords while the melody is played or sung. Listen carefully to the sound.

At the end of the above melody there are two endings (⌐1.⎯⎯⎯⎯⎯⌐ and ⌐2.⎯⎯⎯⎯⎯⌐). Notice the double bar at the end of each ending. The two dots on the staff at the end of the first ending are *repeat marks* indicating that the melody is repeated from the beginning. However, the first ending is omitted in the repetition and the second ending concludes the melody. These two endings avoid recopying the music when the repetition is identical except for a different cadence or ending.

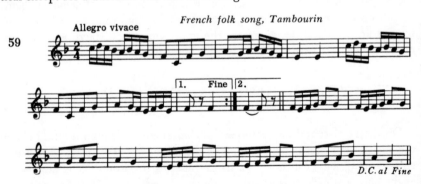

Here again there are two distinct endings. Above the first ending is the word *Fine* which means "end or termination." At the end of the melody are the initials *DC* which are the abbreviation for *Da Capo,* meaning "from the head" or from the beginning. The *DC* is placed at the end to indicate that the performer must return to the beginning and conclude at the *Fine* sign. The full term is *Da Capo al Fine.* We sing the melody through the first ending, and the repeat marks (:|) indicate a repetition from the beginning. This time the first ending is omitted and the second ending is used. The melody continues on to the *Da Capo* where there is a return to the beginning and the close of the melody is at the *Fine* sign at the first ending.

In some of the following melodies, the lowest number in the time signature indicates that the eighth note receives one beat. Thus the quarter note receives two beats, the dotted quarter three beats and so on. We can add 2/8, 3/8, and 4/8 to our list of *simple meters.*

Here are some skips of the I and V chords taken from the context of the melodies. Sing these in all keys with letter names and accidentals.

60

MELODIES FOR SINGING AND DICTATION

1. Brahms, Cradle Song

Not too slow

2. Schubert, "Unfinished" Symphony

Allegro moderato

3. Mozart, Finale

4. French folk song

5. German folk song

6. Hymn tune

7. German folk song

8. German folk song

9. German folk song

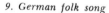

10. German folk song

11. French folk song

12. British folk song

13. Dutch folk song

14. French folk song

Moderato

16. Old French song

Brightly

17. French folk song

Allegretto

18. German folk song

Andante

19. Polish carol

Quietly

20. German folk song

Moderato

21. W. Otto Meissner

Waltz

22. Beethoven, Symphony No. 9

Allegro

23. Bach, Gloria from B Minor Mass

24. Beethoven, Piano Sonata Op. 53, last movement

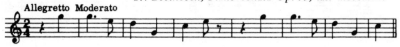

25. German folk song

26. British folk song

27. W. Otto Meissner

28. Giardini, Italian hymn

The Dominant Seventh Chord

Sterkel

61

Sing this melody noticing the outline of the chords. In measure 2-3 the V chord is outlined (D, F sharp, and A) and another tone on the next space is added to the triad.

62

Since there are seven tones between the D and the C of the chord, it is called a V7 chord. The skips of the V7 are often used in melodies both ascending and descending. Hear the V and V7 chords played on the piano. Note that the V7 chord, because of the added 7th, has more of a feeling of expectancy or unrest than the V chord and, therefore, demands satisfaction or resolution. The 7th of the V7 (C) has a very strong tendency to resolve or progress down a step to B.

Sing the following pattern using letter names and accidentals.

63

I   V7   I

This pattern should also be sung to gain experience in other skips of the V7.

64

Drink to Me Only with Thine Eyes

65

Sing this familiar song and notice the rhythmic pattern. Previously, we have sung melodies in simple meters where all the pulses were subdivided by two or its multiples. In this melody, you will find there are only two underlying or principal pulses in each measure, which are themselves divided into smaller units or groupings of three. This division of the beat into three or its multiples is called *compound meter*. The time signature here is 6/8. Within the two pulses, there are six beats to a measure (three beats to each of the pulses). The eighth note receives one beat. How many beats do the ♩ and ♩. receive? Since the tempo is relatively slow, the six beats are felt individually. However, the over-all pulse is still two main stresses to a measure. When the tempo is quick, the two pulses become more prominent. The conducting outline is either:

66 for the six beats in the measure, or **67** for the two main pulses.

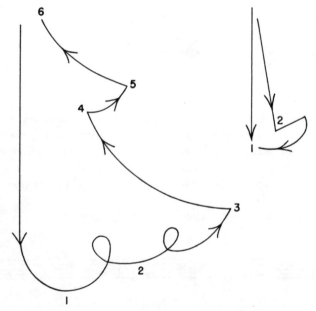

Table of simple meters *

Duple: 2/4; 2/2; 2/8
Triple: 3/4; 3/2; 3/8
Quadruple: 4/4; 4/2; 4/8

Table of compound meters

Duple: 6/8; 6/4; 6/2
Triple: 9/8; 9/4; 9/2
Quadruple: 12/8; 12/4

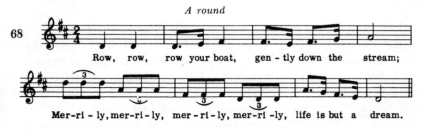

68

A round

Row, row, row your boat, gen - tly down the stream;

Mer-ri - ly, mer-ri - ly, mer - ri - ly, mer-ri -ly, life is but a dream.

Sing this familiar *round* and pay particular attention to the rhythm. There are two beats to the measure in simple meter. In measures 5 and 6, there are three notes to each pulse, which causes an irregular division of the beat in 2/4 meter. Notice the three notes are joined together by a curved line with the number three under it, indicating that the three notes are to be performed in the usual time of two notes of like value. Here they are equal in value to one beat (♩). This rhythmic figure is called a *triplet*. A *triplet*

69   ♫♩ = ♩
        3

occurs when a beat, in any meter where the quarter note is the unit of measurement, is divided into three parts.

Foster, Old Folks at Home

70

Way down up - on the Swa - nee riv - er,

Far, far a - way, There's where my heart is

turn - ing ev - er There's where the old folks stay.

---

* For rare time signatures consult any standard reference work.

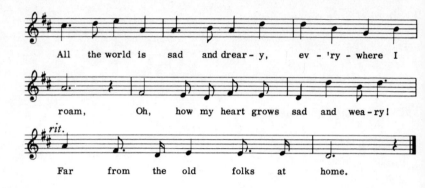

All the world is sad and drear-y, ev - 'ry - where I

roam, Oh, how my heart grows sad and wea-ry!

Far from the old folks at home.

In singing and conducting this Stephen Foster song, you will find in measures 2 and 6 a change in the expected pulse. This is an extremely effective rhythmic device, and is called *syncopation*. Examples in syncopation were found in melodies in Chapter 4. Here, in this melody, it is more obvious, since the beat is divided. In measure 2, the stress is on the second syllable of "riv-er," which is normally a weak beat. Thus the 4th beat of measure 2 is deprived of its regular stress. The stress comes between the regular beat of the measure, and sets up a mild disturbance from the regular recurring pulse. Conduct as you sing and notice where the pulse falls.

MELODIES FOR SINGING AND DICTATION

1. Mozart, Eine Kleine Nachtmusik, third movement

2. Mexican folk song, The Incognito Gallant

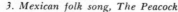

3. Mexican folk song, The Peacock

4. Danish folk song, Good Evening

5. Danish singing game

6. Folk game song, Big Bunch, Little Bunch. Collected by John W. Work

7. Singing game

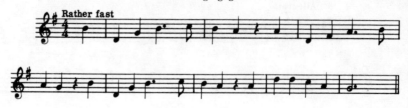

8. Adam de la Halle, Robin Loves Me

9. Hallelujah, I'm a Bum

10. Canadian folk song

a tempo

11. Texas song, Will You Come to the Bow'r?

12. Sea chanty, The Rio Grande

67

13. 14th century German carol

14. Widdecombe Fair

15. Cockles and Mussels

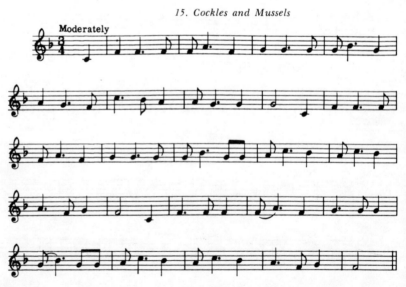

16. Folk song

17. Mozart, Allegro from Divertimento

18. Beethoven, God in Nature

19. Mozart, Passepied

69

20. *Rossini*

21. *Schubert, Hark! Hark! the Lark*

22. *Adam de la Halle, Robin and Marion*

23. *American folk song, Polly Wolly Doodle*

24. German folk song

25. Folk song

26. Gounod, Sanctus from St. Cecilia Mass

27. Handel, He Shall Feed His Flock, from the Messiah

71

28. Tschaikowski, Symphony No. 5

29. German folk song

30. Schubert

31. Maine

32. Danish folk song

33. *Muffat*

34. *Spanish folk song*

35. *English folk song*

36. *Handel, Duet from Solomon*

37. *Bach, Gigue from French Suite No. 6*

73

38. Singing game

39. Antoine Dauvergne

40. Folk song of Chile

41. Chabrier, Habanera

42. *Italian folk song*

43. *Beethoven, Symphony No. 7*

44. *Polish Christmas carol*

45. *Capstan chanty, Shenandoah*

46. *17th century English melody*

75

The Subdominant Chord

Norwegian folk song

71

As you sing this folk song notice the skips of the chord tones. In the first two measures the I chord is outlined in the melody (C-E-G). In the third measure we find the skips (F-A-C) which fall on adjacent lines and spaces on the staff. In referring to the scale of triads, we see that F (the root of the triad) is the fourth degree of the scale, hence the *IV chord* in the key of C.

72

I   IV

Sing the following I-IV-I pattern with letter names and accidentals in all keys. The IV often progresses to the I chord.

73

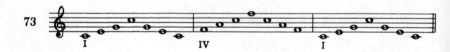

I   IV   I

German folk song

74

In this melody the IV chord is outlined in measure 2 and is followed by the V7 in the next measure. Sing the progression I-IV-V7 I with letter names and accidentals in all keys. This is another frequently used progression.

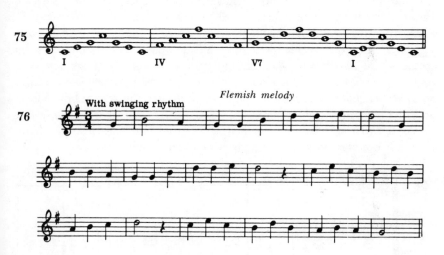

75

76

Flemish melody

Sing this melody and analyze for scale-wise progressions, repeated tones, and skips of chord tones. Spell the I, IV, and V7 chords in the key of G and sing them in arpeggio form. Using only the root of each chord (G, C, or D), let us sing another part with the melody. This supplies a simple accompaniment to the melody and outlines the harmonic background. By hearing and testing the melody and the accompaniment at the piano, decide where the three chords sound best.

Here is one harmonization of the melody with the chords added in the bass clef. Notice there is only one chord used in each measure.

Sing the root of each chord as the melody is being played. We soon see in our analysis that certain tones in the melody do not belong to the underlying chord or harmony. These are called *non-harmonic* or *non-chord tones*. In the first measure the tone A is not included in the I chord (GBD). Since it passes down from a tone of the chord to another tone of the chord, it is called a *passing tone*. Find the other passing tones in the melody. Some passing tones are on the accented beat and some are unaccented passing tones. In measure 3 the tone E is not included in the I chord. Since this tone progresses up a step from a tone of the chord and returns to the same tone, it is called an *upper neighbor tone*. Find the other neighbor tones in the melody. There are other kinds of non-chord tones; we will discuss them as they appear in the music. In order to determine whether a tone is a chord tone or a non-chord tone, it is necessary to know the underlying chord or harmony.

Here is a simple accompaniment of the melody in waltz rhythm. Sing the melody while the accompaniment is being played on the piano. Notice that the tones of successive chords in the right hand part either progress to the nearest tones (no skips) or are common tones and are repeated. The only skips are in the bass or left hand part. The root is doubled in all the chords and the fifth is omitted in the V7 to make a smoother progression.

Write these chords in various keys for practice.

79

German folk song

80

In this melody, the chords or harmony for each measure are suggested underneath. Check these by singing and hearing them on the piano. Where are the non-chord tones? The D in measure 4 is repeated from the previous measure. This is a delayed tone which does not change when the chord changes, and then resolves or moves to a tone of the chord. This non-chord tone is called a *suspension*. In the last measure the G is a non-chord tone and is reached by a skip. It resolves down a step to a chord tone. This tone introduced by a skip and resolved stepwise is called an *appoggiatura*. Here we have two more non-chord tones.

We have now sung and analyzed melodies using the I, IV, V and V7 chords. The I, IV, and V chords are called the primary triads or chords and are the ones most often used in music. Triads can be built on all the other degrees of the scale, but these serve as substitutes for these three primary triads to give variety and contrast to the music.

Terms

Con expressione: With expression.
Vivace: Lively, brisk.
Cantabile: In a melodious, singing style.
Pastorale: Soft movement in a pastoral style.
Con moto: With motion, not dragging.
Scherzando: Playful, lively, merry.

Practice these skips of the IV chord taken from the melodies of this chapter. Sing them in all keys.

81

MELODIES FOR SINGING AND DICTATION

1. W. Otto Meissner, Old Dobbin

2. W. Otto Meissner

3. Dutch folk song

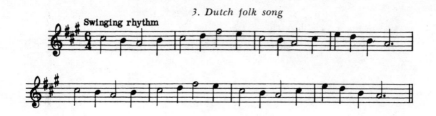

4. French folk song—Le Roi d'Yvetot

5. German folk song

6. German folk song

81

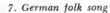
7. German folk song

8. Creole folk song

9. Philippine folk song

10. Beethoven

11. German folk song

12. German folk song

13. Pierce Gaveaux

14. Bach, Minuet

Allegretto   *15. Norwegian folk song, Paul on the Hill*

16. Haydn, Quartet No. 74

17. Norwegian folk song

Moderate time

84

18. American singing game

19. Beethoven

20. Franz, For Music

21. W. Otto Meissner

22. Finnish folk song

23. Russian folk song

24. English folk song

25. Russian folk song

26. W. Otto Meissner

Moderato

27. Traditional

Allegro

28. Bishop, Home Sweet Home

In moderate time

rit.

29. Foster, My Old Kentucky Home

Chorus

rit.

30. English folk song

Con expressione

31. W. Otto Meissner

Moderato

32. Brahms, From Volks Kinderlieder

Con moto ... **Fine**

D.C. al Fine

33. French folk song

Dance tune ... **Fine**

D.C. al Fine

34. English folk song

Moderato

35. Canadian folk song

Allegretto

89

36. Bohemian Christmas carol

37. English folk song

38. British folk song

39. W. Otto Meissner

40. English folk song

41. English folk song

42. Bach, Chorale

43. *Haydn*

With dignity

44. *Mozart, Air from Bastien and Bastienne*

Allegro moderato

45. *Beethoven, Trio in B♭, third movement*

Andante cantabile

92

The Minor Mode

82

In this excerpt from "The Heavens Are Telling" from Haydn's *Creation*, we find all the tones of the C major scale in the first four measures. In the remaining part of the melody, several flats (accidentals) are added which give variety and color to the melody. These altered tones are the *third* and *sixth* degrees of the scale (E flat and A flat). When the third and sixth degrees of the major scale are lowered one-half step, the scale becomes *minor*.

83

93

The key tone is C throughout the melody, so there has been no change in the tonality. However, from measure 6 on to the end of the melody, the tones present a different mode, the *minor mode*. The word mode is from the Latin word *modus,* which means style or manner. These tones form the C *minor scale* which is the *parallel scale* to C major, since they both have the same key tone. Thus the keys of C major and C minor are both represented in this melody. Sing this minor scale several times and write other minor scales from their parallel major scales. A composer will often use the parallel major and minor alternately in his compositions for harmonic and melodic variety. It is a "borrowing" of the tones from the parallel key, and is an effective device.

Sing and analyze the above melody. Here again the third and sixth degrees are lowered from the parallel major scale of C. This is called the *harmonic minor scale,* and is most often used as the basis for harmonic treatment. The pitches are the same both ascending and descending.

In the above melody, the accidentals (flats) are placed with the notes instead of the key signature. When a melody is in the minor mode, it is desirable to have a key signature which will avoid as much as possible the constant use of accidentals. In this melody, a key signature is needed which contains an E flat and an A flat. The closest signature and the one causing the fewest accidentals is the E flat major signature, which has three flats

86 &. A natural sign is used for the B, and the lowered 3rd and 6th steps are taken care of by the key signature. Notice that the key signature for

C minor is the same as for E flat major. These are called *relative keys*. The
third degree of the minor scale (E flat) is the key tone of the relative major
scale. Each major and minor scale has its relative scale. Thus:

Sing this melody and notice the scale-wise progressions. The melody begins and ends on C. What is the key? The E flat (third note) in the melody
sets up the minor feeling immediately. In measure 2, the first four tones are
the 5th, 6th and 7th degrees of the scale, and are the same as those degrees
in the parallel key (C major). Thus, except for the E flat, this minor scale
ascending is the same as the parallel major scale. Referring to measure 2
again, the 6th and 7th degrees descending are lowered (B flat and A flat)
from the parallel major. This is the *melodic minor scale,* and is used more
often melodically. Notice how closely the ascending scale resembles the
parallel major scale, thus:

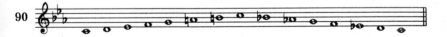

With the use of the key signature for C minor, accidentals are needed to
raise the 6th and 7th degrees, thus:

90

95

91

In singing and hearing this melody, you will immediately know that it is in C minor. But the sound is somewhat different from that in our other minor melodies. The B flat in measures 2 and 6 gives a special flavor to the music. The other minor scales have one half step between the 7th and 8th degrees of the scale ascending; here there is a whole step. Here are the tones in the melody in scale-wise order ascending and descending:

92

Notice the tones of the scale ascending and descending are the same as the descending form of the melodic scale. This scale is called the *natural minor scale,* and has its origin in the old Aeolian mode, which corresponds to the white keys on the piano from A to A. The modes were the predecessors of our present major and minor scale and formed the basis of Western music until the seventeenth century. The study of these old church modes, as they were called, and the transition to our present-day major and minor scales is fascinating. Composers still use modal effects in their music though the modes have been superseded by our scales.*

Here is a summary and comparison of the three kinds of minor scales. Notice the 6th and 7th degrees of the scales are the ones which are altered. The lowered 3rd degree is the same in all the scales. Write and sing these scales so you can easily recognize them when they appear in your music.

---

* See Howard A. Murphy and Edwin J. Stringham, *Creative Harmony and Musicianship* (Englewood Cliffs, N.J.: Prentice-Hall, Inc., 1951).

Here is a folk song with a second part or melody added. Sing and notice the skips and step-wise progressions. The upper melody in the first two measures is the descending major scale. The lower or second part is stationary. Let us now consider the interval relationship between the voices vertically. The distance on the staff between two tones is an interval, and when the two tones are sounded simultaneously, they form a *harmonic interval*. In our study of the major scale, we discovered that some of the intervals were whole steps and some were half steps (Chapter Two, p. 13). These were *melodic intervals* as they progressed horizontally. We are now concerned with discovering the interval relationship between the stationary C of the second or lower part of the melody (which is the key tone of C major) and each tone of the major scale (the upper melody). These intervals all have names and here is the chart of the intervals within the key ascending. The sign for major is +, for minor −, and P means a perfect interval.

From this chart, we can conclude that the interval from the key tone of a major scale to any other tone of the scale is either a *perfect* or *major interval*. To find the name of any melodic or harmonic interval, consider the lowest tone as the key tone of a major scale. If the upper tone is a tone within that major scale, it is, therefore, either major or perfect as shown in the chart above. If it is not in the scale, then it is altered in some way and has another name. For example, sing and hear these two intervals:

96

They are similar since they are both thirds (C to E). Hence the *quantity* of the interval is the same. However, the sound is not the same, so the *quality* is different between the two. What is the quality? According to the plan in the previous paragraph, we consider C as the key tone of C major. Since E natural is in the scale of C, by referring to the chart of intervals, we find it is a major third. In the second interval the E flat is used. Thus the major third is lowered one-half step, making it a *minor interval*. The quantity of the two intervals is the same, but the quality differs. Major and perfect intervals may be altered thus:

Major intervals

If a major interval is lowered one-half step, it becomes a *minor interval:*

97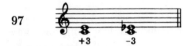

If it is raised one-half step, it becomes *augmented:*

98

If a major interval is lowered one whole step, it becomes *diminished:*

99

Perfect intervals

If a perfect interval is raised one-half step, it becomes *augmented:*

100

If it is lowered one-half step, it becomes *diminished:*

101

Locate and name all the other harmonic intervals in the two-part example above.

Just as in the major keys, the triads on I, IV and V are often outlined melodically in minor keys. In the melody below, the I chord is outlined in measures 2-3, and the V chord in measures 5-6. Notice that the harmonic form of the minor scale is used.

102

Polish folk song

Moderato

Sing the I, IV and V7 chords in all minor keys in arpeggio form using letter names and accidentals. Notice again the lowered third and sixth degrees of the parallel major scale. Listen to the difference in sound in major and minor.

103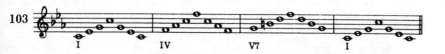

Let us now check the difference in quality between the triads or chords in a major and a minor key. Here are the chords in major:

104

The I chord has a major third and a perfect fifth from its root. This is a *major chord.* The IV and V chords have the same quality, so they are also *major chords.* The V7 chord has a major triad and a minor 7th (G to F).

This added seventh gives the chord a feeling of tension or restlessness which demands a resolution to another chord. Thus, it is called a *dissonant chord.* The major and minor triads or chords give a feeling of satisfaction or rest in themselves and do not demand this resolution. These are called *consonant chords.**

Here are the I, IV, V and V7 chords in minor:

105

The I chord has a minor third and a perfect fifth. This forms a *minor triad.* The IV chord is also *minor.* The V and V7 are the same as in major.

Terms

Grazioso: In a graceful style.
Sostenuto: Sustaining the tone.
Molto tranquillo: Calm, quiet.
Grave: Slow and solemn.
Assez lent: Rather slowly.

MELODIES FOR SINGING AND DICTATION

1. Russian folk song

---

* Intervals are also classified as *consonant* or *dissonant.* The perfect intervals are called *perfect consonants,* the minor and major thirds and sixths, imperfect consonants. All the others are *dissonant.*

2. Roumanian folk song, *Ice Upon the River*

3. Brahms, *Longings*

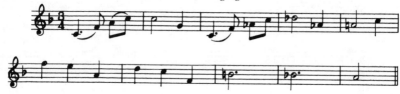

4. Strauss, *Night*

5. Brahms, The Vain Suit

6. Yiddish folk song, Lullaby

7. Ukrainian folk song, Letter Writer

8. Russian folk song, Charm

9. Italian folk song, Mother, the Bells are Ringing

10. Swedish folk song, Perhaps When Lilies Bloom

11. Swedish folk song, I Sit Alone

12. German folk song, Count and Nun

13. American folk song, Putney Hymn

14. Rumanian folk song, Ardeleana

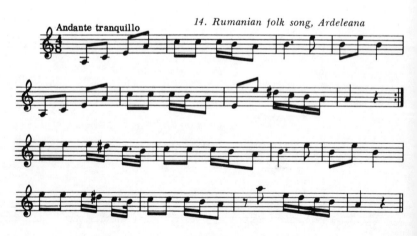

15. Hudson River Ballad, Ballad of Henry Green

16. Swedish folk song, Joy in Heaven

17. Swedish folk song, It Cannot Be

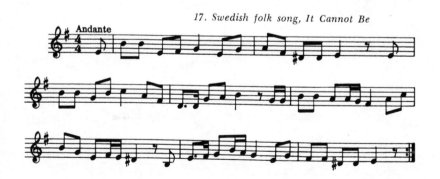

18. Swedish folk song, All Day While I'm at Work

19. Canadian folk song, O Little Rock

20. Canadian folk song, And I Would Flee Away

21. Coventry Carol, 17th century

22. Negro spiritual

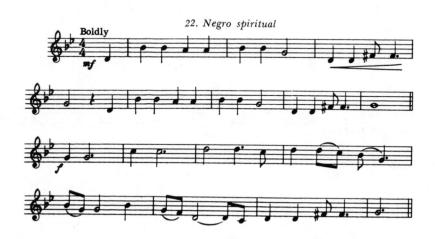

23. Yiddish folk song, Hannukkah

24. Old French Carol, Masters in This Hall

Brightly

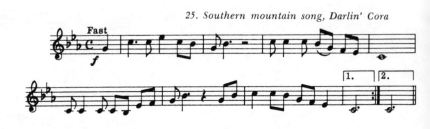

25. Southern mountain song, Darlin' Cora

Fast

26. Ancient European folk song, Who is the Man?

Moderato

27. Welsh folk song, The Grey Old Stone

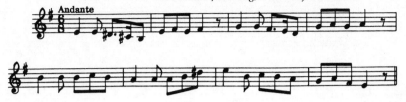

28. Negro ballad, The Lonesome Road

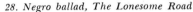

29. Thomas Casey, Drill, Ye Tarriers, Drill

30. British folk song

31. *Beethoven, Concerto for Violin*

32. *Schumann, Symphony No. 1*

Allegro animato

33. *Dvorak, "New World" Symphony*

34. *Dvorak, Slavonic Dance*

35. *French folk song*

Allegretto

36. Irish folk song

37. Polish folk song

38. Mozart, Symphony No. 40, first movement

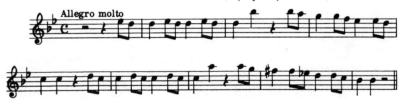

39. Finnish folk song

40. Finnish folk song

41. Dvorak, "New World" Symphony, first movement

42. Bach, Chorale melody

43. Gabriel, Marie, La Cinquantine

44. Liszt, Tarantella

45. Swedish folk song

46. German folk song

47. Russian folk song

48. Bach, Chorale melody

9

Modulation to the Dominant Key and Implied Modulation

So far, in our study and analysis, each melody has remained in the same tonality and key. One way of gaining variety and contrast in music is by moving from one tonality to another, that is, changing the key tone. This change of tonality is called *modulation.*

Mozart, Minuet from Don Giovanni

106

Hear this *minuet* several times. Notice that it begins in the tonality of C major and ends in G major. The first four measures are in the key of C. The I and V chords firmly establish this tonality. In measure 5 the chord outline is D, F sharp, and A. This is the first chord not in the original tonality and suggests to the ear the possibility of a new key. In measure 6 the chord is G-/B-/D. The two successive chords, therefore, are V7 to I in G major.

114

These two chords, however, are not sufficient in themselves to establish a new key or tonality. Our ears need a strong cadence or ending in the new key, as we have here, to confirm and set up the new tonality. The V7 of the new key is a most valuable and common chord in modulating from one key to another. Notice that in the modulation from C to G, we move up to the fifth degree of the scale. This is the dominant tone and it is a *dominant modulation*. It is the most frequent one in music. It will be helpful to think of this modulation in three parts:

1. Establish the original key or tonality, I-V7-I in C major.
2. Progress to the new key, V7 to I in G.
3. Confirm the new key with a cadence or ending in G major.

107

Sing this melody and notice the modulation from E flat to B flat major. The first five measures establish the key of E flat. In measure 6, the V7 of the new key (B flat) is outlined in the melody (F-A-C-E flat). This new key of B flat is then established and confirmed by the last two measures. Here is an outline of this modulation:

E flat (I V7 I) B flat (V7 I V7 I)

Sing this modulation in arpeggio form in all major keys with letter names and accidentals.

108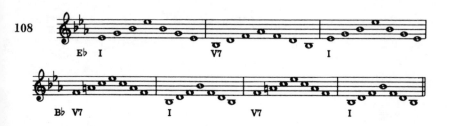

The following melodies modulate to the dominant key (the fifth degree of the original key). Analyze each one for the modulatory chord. Sing the V7 on all tones so you will become very familiar with its sound. You will find many different kinds of modulations in music, but remember that, unless a new tonality is established, a modulation is impossible.

MELODIES FOR SINGING AND DICTATION

1. Folk song

Allegretto

2. Kreipl

With spirit

3. Folk song

4. Methfessel

Not too fast

5. Folk song

Allegro moderato

6. Zelter

Moderato

7. Silcher

Andante

8. Himmel

Andante

117

9. Eberwein

10. Hurka

11. Caron

12. Folk song

13. Folk song

14. Russian folk song

15. Kreutzer

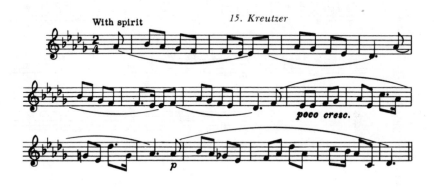

16. Weber, Der Freischutz

17. Anonymous

18. Chorale, Meisterchorale No. 19

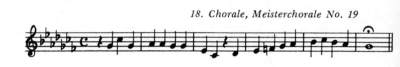

19. Dutch folk song

20. Sullivan, The Mikado

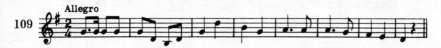

In this melody, we see no accidentals (sharp, flat or natural signs) to give
a hint of a possible modulation. But the ending of the melody gives a feeling
of being the scale-line 54321 of the dominant key of D major. So often this
short and sudden modulation is in the middle of a melody. The use of chords
and harmony to support the melody aids considerably in implying the brief
change of tonality. However, even in the case of unharmonized melodies,
the dominant tonality is apparent. A modulation where there is no accidental
to indicate the change of tonality is an *implied modulation*.

MELODIES FOR SINGING AND DICTATION

4. Capstan chanty, Yeo, Heave, Ho!

5. Mozart, Ballet Suite

6. Sullivan, Patience

7. Haydn, Symphony in C Minor

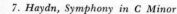

8. Sullivan, The Mikado

9. Chorale melody, Meisterchorale No. 19

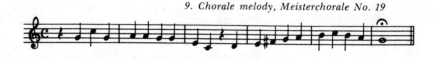

10. August Pohlenz

11. Mozart, Bundeslied

12. Schumann, Bronco

13. British folk song

14. Kuhlau, Rondo Op. 40, No. 2

15. Dutch folk song

16. Haydn, Minuetto

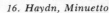

17. Sullivan, The Mikado

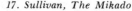

18. Bach, Chorale melody

19. Beethoven

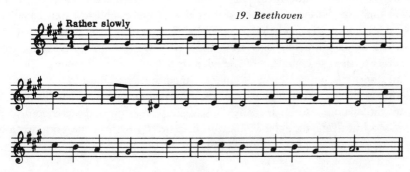

Chromaticism

Moskowski, Spanish Dance

110

Sing and analyze this dance melody. Notice that in several places sharps are placed before the notes. These "new" tones are not included in the regular tones of the C major scale. Also, they do not establish a new tonality or modulation as the melodies in Chapter 9. Therefore, these are called *chromatic tones. Chromaticism* (from the Greek word, *chroma,* meaning color) refers to the use of tones not included in the prevailing diatonic scale. They are tones foreign to the scale and are modifications of the scale tones. The tone is altered either higher or lower (sharped or flatted). Usually the tones of the diatonic scale are raised ascending and lowered descending. The raised fourth degree (the F sharp in measure 6) is the same both ascending and descending. This is the only exception.

Chromatic scale of C

111

Sing and write the chromatic scale in other keys for practice. These tones are added to the diatonic ones to give variety and color. They "embellish" the tones within the scale.

In the following melodies determine if the chromatic tones are embellishing tones or part of a modulation. The ear is always the final judge in this decision. A few supporting chords as an accompaniment will help the ear.

MELODIES FOR SINGING AND DICTATION

1. Schubert

2. Mozart, Berceuse

3. Mexican folk song

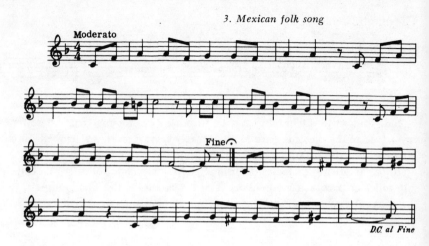

Moderato

Fine

D.C. al Fine

4. Russian gypsy tune

Waltz time

5. Dutch folk song

Andante

6. British folk song

Allegretto

7. German folk song

Moderato

8. Haydn, Austrian hymn

Majestically

9. Slovakian folk song, Water Running

Andante

10. Hudson River Song, The Weeping Willow

Slowly

11. Danish folk song, Good Evening, My Pretty

Andante

12. Flat River Girl

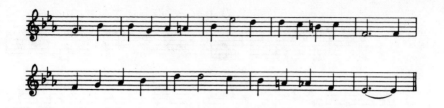

13. A. A. Melville, Genesee River Song

14. H. P. Danks, Genesee River Song

15. German folk song, *Now We Must Part*

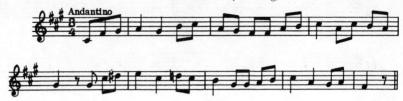

16. Delaware River Song, *Ben Bolt*

17. Sea chanty, *One More Day*

18. German folk song

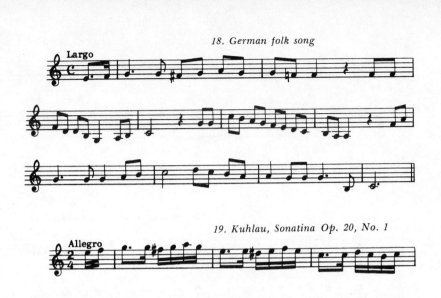

19. Kuhlau, Sonatina Op. 20, No. 1

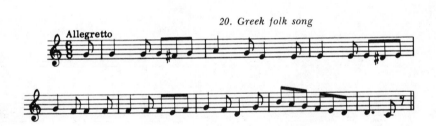

20. Greek folk song

21. Mozart, Ave Verum

22. Mozart, Symphony in G Major

23. Mozart, Piano Sonata K331

24. J. Strauss, You and Me Waltz

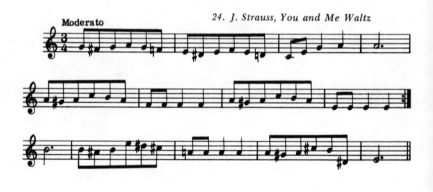

25. von Pothko

26. Schumann, Album for the Young

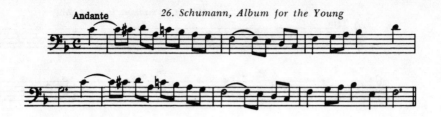

27. Dussek, Rondo

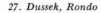

28. Mozart, Gavotte

29. Mozart, Eine Kleine Nachtmusik, third movement

30. Mozart, Symphony in G Major

31. Himmel

Andante con moto

32. Himmel

Allegro moderato

33. Folk song

Allegretto

34. Sullivan, Pirates of Penzance

Allegro vivace

35. Bach

36. Schumann, March from Carnaval, Op. 9

37. Sullivan, Pirates of Penzance

Allegro vivace

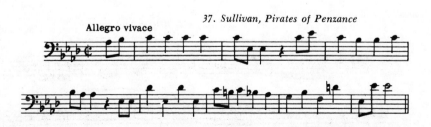

38. Himmel

39. Folk song

40. Greek folk song

41. British folk song

42. Bach

Slowly

43. German folk song

Slowly

erms

Forzando: With force, energy.
Bravura: Boldness, brilliance.
Energia: With energy and decision.
Expressione: With feeling.
Brio: Spirit, fire.
Dolce: Sweetly
Maestoso: With majesty and dignity.
Fuoro: Fire, spirit.
Mezzo piano: Medium soft.

139

Form in Music

We have now discussed some of the materials of music which are available to the composer. It is most important that we turn our attention to the plan and organization of these materials in musical compositions. It is necessary that we discover how a composer, using the basic materials of rhythm, harmony and melody, arranges and develops his ideas in order to give them meaning and significance. The resulting design or structure is called *form* in music.

Even though the structure of a composition may be quite individual in its plan, and often the specific type of music sets up its own form or design, there are certain established structures or forms which seem to offer a natural pattern or plan for presenting the composer's ideas. Through the years, certain fundamental concepts of organizing music materials have developed. The composer takes these established designs and adapts them to his own needs and feelings. They serve as a stimulus or a support for the composer, and offer a structural mold which he can use in his own way. By studying and understanding these forms and designs, we are better able to follow the composer's thoughts and ideas, and the performance of the music becomes more meaningful and intelligible.

In discussing and analyzing musical forms, we must keep in mind two basic principles necessary for coherence and balance in music. These are unity and variety. Unity is achieved by repetition of material either exact or similar; variety is gained by contrast of material (new melodies and variations of material). In order for music to sound well and have order, it is essential to have a balance between these two general principles. As you listen to music, notice how the composer achieves this unity and variety.

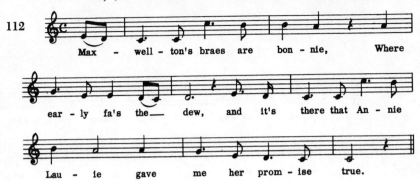

Lady John Scott, Annie Laurie. Words by William Douglas

112

Max - well - ton's braes are bon - nie, Where

ear - ly fa's the— dew, and it's there that An - nie

Lau - ie gave me her prom - ise true.

Sing the first part of the familiar song, *Annie Laurie*. In measure 4 you will hear a pause in the music or the end of a musical thought or idea and the beginning of another one which ends in measure 6. These musical ideas are divided into parts or sections, and the endings of these sections are called *cadences*. Certain groupings are, therefore, set up which make the music more understandable. Without these cadences, the music would be monotonous and rambling.

Sing the first four measures again. We can easily hear this natural pause or temporary stop in the flow of the melody. However, the melody could not end here and express a complete thought. This transient ending is called a *half* or *semi-cadence*. The melody then continues and comes to a complete close. This is a *final* or *full cadence*. Generally speaking, all cadences are classified as *complete* or *incomplete*. Each part of the melody separated by a cadence is called a *phrase* in music. The *phrase* is the basic unit of form, and is comparable to a sentence, although, as we have seen, it need not always present a complete musical idea. But it must be long enough and unified enough to have meaning. Phrases vary in length, but in simple music they are usually four measures, as in our example. Here we have two four-measure phrases. When the first phrase ends on an incomplete cadence, the two phrases combine to form a *period*, as in *Annie Laurie*. Since the second phrase begins with the same melody as the first, it is called a *parallel period*. When the phrases are unlike melodically, they form a *contrasting period*. Here is the outline of the first part of *Annie Laurie*.

Parallel period: Phrase (4 measures) ends on half cadence.

Phrase (4 measures) ends on complete (final) cadence.

141

Sing the first part of *Drink to Me Only with Thine Eyes:*

Old English air, *Drink to Me Only with Thine Eyes.*
Words by Ben Jonson

Drink to me on - ly with__ thine eyes,__ And

I __ will pledge with mine,__ Or leave a` kiss with-

in __ the cup,__ And I'll__ not ask for wine.__

Where is the first phrase? Is the cadence complete or incomplete? Notice the phrase ends with a complete cadence after four measures. The phrase is then repeated exactly note for note. This is, therefore, a *repeated phrase,* not a period. The melody must be the same in a repeated phrase; the harmony can be the same or different.

Gruber, *Silent Night.* Words by Joseph Mohr

Si - lent night, Ho - ly night, All is calm, all is bright

'Round yon Vir - gin Moth-er and Child, Ho - ly In-fant so ten-der and mild,

Sleep in heav-en-ly peace,__ Sleep__ in heav-en-ly peace.__

Sing the Christmas carol *Silent Night,* and notice the cadences and phrases. How many phrases are there, and which cadences are complete and incomplete? Here we find a series of three phrases, the first two ending on incomplete cadences, and the last one on a complete cadence. This is called a *phrase group* and consists of two or three similar or unlike phrases which substitute for the period form.

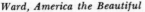

Sing *America the Beautiful*. Analyze the cadences and phrases. Here we find a series of four phrases, the first three ending on incomplete cadences and the fourth on a complete one. This form is called a *double period*. Notice that the double period is divided in half by an *incomplete cadence*.

Here is the beginning of *Beethoven's Symphony No. 5 Op. 67*.

Beethoven, Symphony No. 5

Here we have a simple four-note pattern with a descending third. This presents a musical idea, which is repeated on different notes in the measures following. This short group of tones is called a *motive* or *figure* and the repetition of it on different tones is called a *sequence*.

In singing and analyzing your melodies, always decide on the form of the music. Listen carefully for cadences, phrases, periods, double periods, and the phrase group. We have discussed form in music as it is related to shorter songs and parts of compositions. Let us now consider some of the larger forms in music.

Sing the entire song, *Drink to Me Only with Thine Eyes:*

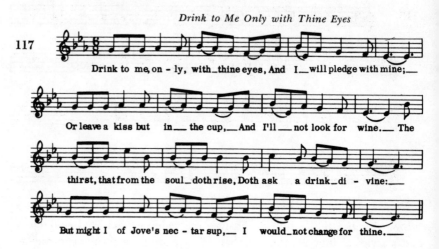

Drink to Me Only with Thine Eyes

117

Drink to me, on - ly, with thine eyes, And I will pledge with mine;

Or leave a kiss but in the cup, And I'll not look for wine. The

thirst, that from the soul doth rise, Doth ask a drink di - vine:

But might I of Jove's nec - tar sup, I would not change for thine.

We have already discovered that the first four measures form a phrase, which is repeated. The next four measures present a new phrase (new melody) which ends on a half or semi-cadence. The first phrase is then repeated again. Here is the outline of the form:

A: Phrase (repeated) ends on complete cadence.
B: Phrase ends on half cadence.
A: Phrase ends on complete cadence.

This is a most common form in music: *the three-part* or *ternary form* (A-B-A). This form was discovered in our melodies in Chapter 2. It illustrates most clearly and simply the idea of unity and variety in music. The repetition of part A gives unity to the song, while the new material of part B offers the needed variety. The last repetition of part A gives balance and unity and a sense of completeness.

Brahms, Lullaby

Andante

118

Sing and analyze the *Brahms' Cradle Song*. Where is the first complete cadence? The first eight measures present part A and the rest of the song is new material (B). There is no return to A here, so it is a two-part or binary form (AB). In order to have the needed balance, part B often resembles part A either rhythmically or melodically.

119

Way down up - on the Swa - nee riv - er,

Far, far a - way, There's where my heart is

turn - ing ev - er There's where the old folks stay.

All the world is sad and drear - y, ev - 'ry - where I

roam, Oh, how my heart grows sad and wea - ry!

rit.

Far from the old folks at home.

Here is the song, *Swanee River*. Notice again the phrases and cadences. Here, again, is the three-part form. However, part A is a period and parts B and the repetition of A are phrases. It is common practice in the folk song to use the second phrase of part A as the third part of the three-part form, as in our example. Here is the outline of the form:

A: (parallel period) First phrase ends on half cadence; second phrase ends on complete cadence.
B: Phrase ends on incomplete cadence.
A: Phrase ends on complete cadence.

In both of our folk songs, the parts were either phrases or periods. If the forms are enlarged, they take on added meaning and become more complex in design. Not only do folk songs follow this three-part idea, but piano pieces, movements of symphonies, sonatas, and so on often follow the same plan. As you listen to music, be aware of its form and design. You will find this will enhance and focus your listening.

Schumann, Bagatelle from Album for the Young

Listen to this short piano piece, *Bagatelle*, from the *Album for the Young* by Robert Schumann. As you listen analyze the over-all form, cadences, and phrases. After you have studied it carefully, compare your analysis with the following outline of the form.

A: (parallel period) First phrase (measures 1-4) ends on half cadence; second phrase (measures 4-8) ends on complete cadence.

B: Phrase (measures 8-12) ends on half cadence (this is same figure used in A).

A: Phrase (measures 12-16) ends on complete cadence.

This is, therefore, a three-part song form (A-B-A). Note the second time A appears, only the second phrase of the original period is used. The repeat signs indicate that parts B and A are repeated again. This immediate repetition of the material does not change the form. This is an important principle of form in music.

Examples of the three-part form are:

1. Mendelssohn, *Songs without Words*

   a) *Venetian Boat Song, No. 2*, Op. 30, No. 6

   b) *Sadness of Soul*, Op. 53, No. 4

2. Schumann, *The Merry Peasant* from *Album for the Young*

3. Chopin, *Mazurka*, Op. 23, No. 3

4. Grieg, *Norwegian Dance*

The three-part form is often combined and expanded into larger and more detailed forms.* The most familiar one is the sonata-allegro form, which is commonly used in the first movements of symphonies, sonatas, and so on, and has served as a basic plan for the creative efforts of many composers.*

---

* Other extended forms are the five-part form, the song form and trio, and the rondos. These forms are discussed and representative music is analyzed in *Lessons in Musical Form* by Percy Goetschius (Oliver Ditson Company).

The form was established in the Classic period with Haydn, Mozart, and Beethoven.

Here is the basic outline of the sonata-allegro form. The key scheme is typical of the form in a major key.*

Exposition:
Principal theme in tonic key
Subordinate theme in dominant key
Closing theme or section in dominant key

Development:
Some or all the themes are developed. Sometimes new material appears.

Recapitulation:
Principal theme in tonic key
Subordinate theme in tonic key
Closing theme in tonic key
Coda

Thus, in the first section (exposition), the material for the movement is presented: the principal theme, the subordinate theme, and the closing theme or section. In the development section, the composer presents some or all of the themes in various designs, keys, sequences, and so on. He is free to use the thematic material of the exposition as he wishes. The recapitulation presents the themes again and adds a coda or extended ending. Notice the key scheme of the form. The subordinate theme in the exposition is in the dominant key but appears in the tonic key in the recapitulation.

Listen to the first movement of *Eine Kleine Nachtmusik* by Mozart. Pay particular attention to the themes, extra material (transitions), key changes, and sections. Check your analysis with the following outline of the form of this movement.

Exposition:
Principal theme in G major, measures 1-18
Transition or extra material (non-thematic), measures 18-27
Subordinate theme in D major, measures 28-35
Closing theme in D major with extended cadence, measures 35-55

Development:
The principal and closing themes are developed here with a transition back to the recapitulation

---

* In a minor movement, the subordinate theme in the exposition is in the relative major key.

Recapitulation:
  Principal theme in G major, measures 76-93
  Transition or extra material, measures 93-101
  Subordinate theme in G major, measures 101-108
  Closing theme in G major, measures 108-128
  Coda, measure 128 to end

We have now analyzed and examined a great amount of music. We have become aware of the symbols of music, its plan and structure. We have discovered its many possibilities and have developed considerable skill and ability in understanding and responding to the printed page and in listening to music. It is hoped that this brief introduction to the many facets of music will serve as a guide and background for continued interest, study, and enjoyment of music.